Tales from the Arabian Nights

Level 2

Retold by Anne Collins
Series Editors: Andy Hopkins and Jocelyn Potter

D1354728

Pearson Education Limited
Edinburgh Gate, Harlow,
Essex CM20 2JE, England
and Associated Companies throughout the world.

ISBN: 978-1-4058-5539-6

First published by Penguin Books 2000
This edition published 2008

7 9 10 8

Text copyright © Penguin Books Ltd 2000
This edition copyright © Pearson Education Ltd 2008
Illustrations by Per Dahlberg

Typeset by Graphicraft Ltd, Hong Kong
Set in 11/14pt Bembo
Printed in China
SWTC/07

Penguin Books Ltd a Penguin Random House company

For a complet~~e list of the titles available~~ to your local
Pearson Longman office or to: Penguin Readers Marketing Department, Pearson Education,
Edinburgh Gate, Harlow, Essex CM20 2JE, England.

Contents

		page
Introduction		v
Chapter 1	The Sultan and Sheherezade	1
Chapter 2	Behind the Door	2
Chapter 3	Sultan Haroun Laughs	8
Chapter 4	Faisal and the Barber	11
Chapter 5	The Boy Judge	16
Chapter 6	The Dwarf of Basra	20
Chapter 7	Ali Baba and the Forty Thieves	24
Chapter 8	The End of the Forty Thieves	28
Chapter 9	The Thief and the Donkey	32
Chapter 10	Aladdin and the Lamp	35
Activities		41

Introduction

Sheherezade stopped.

'Well?' said the sultan. 'What happened next? What was behind the door?'

'Sir, there's light in the sky,' said Sheherezade. 'You're going to kill me now.'

'But you can't stop there. You have to finish the story.'

Sheherezade is beautiful and clever. She also knows many wonderful stories. Night after night, she tells them to Sultan Shahriar. She always stops in an exciting place, so he wants to hear the end of the story. She knows stories for a thousand and one nights. The Arabic name for these stories (*Alf Leila wa Leila*) means *The Thousand and One Nights*.

The stories in this book are very different. Some are sad and some are funny. Some are exciting. We meet many interesting people – an unhappy young man, a clever servant girl, a boy judge, a stupid barber and forty bad thieves. The stories aren't new, but you can find the same people in the world today – a young man in love, a good friend or a clever young boy.

Everybody enjoys a good story, and before the days of television and cinema stories were very important. The stories in *Tales from the Arabian Nights* are very old. People in Europe first read them in French between 1704 and 1717. They don't come from one place, but from many different countries – the Middle East, India and Pakistan. At that time, Europeans didn't know much about the countries in the Middle East. So these stories were very strange and exciting, and they opened a wonderful new world.

Chapter 1   The Sultan and Sheherezade

Sultan Shahriar had a beautiful wife. She was his only wife and he loved her more than anything in the world.

But the sultan's wife took other men as lovers. One day, the sultan found her with another man. He was very angry and cut off the man's head. Then he cut off his wife's head too.

From that time, the sultan began to hate all women.

'From today,' he said to his vizir *, 'I'll marry a new wife every day. She'll stay with me for one night. Then the next morning, I'll cut off her head. So no woman will hurt me again.'

The vizir had to find a new wife for the sultan every day. But this was a very difficult job. Every family was afraid. No girl wanted to be the sultan's wife for one night and then die. Fathers began to send their daughters away.

The vizir too was afraid. 'What will happen to me?' he thought. 'I can't find any more girls. Perhaps the sultan will kill me too.'

The vizir had two daughters. One of them, Sheherezade, was beautiful and very clever. One day she said, 'Dear Father, please do something for me. It will make me, the sultan and the people very happy.'

'I would like to make everybody happy,' said the vizir. 'What is it, my daughter? Ask, and I will do it for you.'

'Give me to the sultan. I will be his wife,' answered Sheherezade.

The vizir's face turned white. 'Never!' he said. 'The sultan will kill you. I can't do that. Please don't ask me.'

'Please do it,' answered Sheherezade. 'Everything will be all right, you'll see. I want to be the sultan's wife.'

---

* vizir: an important man in Muslim countries at that time; he helped the sultan.

1

The vizir put his head in his hands. He was very unhappy. He loved Sheherezade very much and he didn't want to do this thing. But Sheherezade asked again and again, and in the end the vizir said sadly, 'All right, my daughter. But I don't understand. Why do you want to throw your life away?'

Sheherezade went to her sister, Dunyazade, and told her everything. Dunyazade began to cry, but Sheherezade said, 'Don't cry, dear sister. I don't want to die. Everything will be all right, you'll see. But you have to help me. I want you to sleep in the room with the sultan and me. Wake me up one hour before morning. Say to me, "Please tell me a story." That's all.'

◆

The next day, Sheherezade went with her father to see the sultan. The sultan was very surprised. Why did the vizir want his daughter to be the sultan's wife? But Sheherezade was beautiful and the sultan was very happy with her. So he married her.

That night, Sheherezade said to the sultan, 'Sir, please can my sister stay with me tonight – my last night?'

'All right,' said the sultan.

Nobody slept that night. The sultan always slept badly. Sheherezade was excited and Dunyazade was afraid.

One hour before morning, Dunyazade spoke.

'Dear sister,' she said, 'please tell me a story.'

So Sheherezade began.

Chapter 2   Behind the Door

Salem's father was very rich. When he died, he left his money and houses to his son. But Salem was young and lost the money very quickly. Then he sold the houses and lost that money too. In the end, he had nothing.

'Dear sister,' she said, *'please tell me a story.'*

He sat in the streets and waited for work. Sometimes he carried things for people.

One day, an old man spoke to him.

'You had a better place in life,' said the old man. 'I can see it in your face. I live with ten other old men in one house. Come and be our servant.'

Salem walked through the city with the old man and they stopped outside the old man's house. Before they went in, the old man turned to Salem and said, 'This house is a very unhappy place. But never ask any questions about that.'

'I'll remember that,' said Salem, and he followed the old man through the door.

The inside of the house was very beautiful. The rooms were large, with floors of different colours. In the middle of the house was a lovely garden with many flowers. Salem could hear the sound of water and birdsong.

Then he heard other sounds. They came from the other old men. The men wore black, and they cried in their rooms.

The first old man took Salem into his room. He showed him a box with pieces of gold inside.

'Use this gold when you buy things for us,' he said.

Salem also saw a door in the old man's room. He wanted to ask, 'What's behind that door?' But you didn't ask questions in that house.

Salem worked hard in the house for many years. One old man after another old man died, and he put them under the ground in the garden. In the end, there was only one old man – Salem's first friend. Then he was ill too.

'I'm going to die, my son,' he said to Salem.

'Then please tell me something,' said Salem. 'Why are you so unhappy? And what's behind the door in your room?'

'I can't tell you that,' said the old man. 'But don't try to open the door. You'll be unhappy every day of your life.'

The old man died. He left the house and his money to Salem. Now Salem was rich again, but he wasn't happy. He thought about the old men and the door. Why were the old men unhappy? What was behind the door?

Salem had to know the answers to these questions. He took a piece of heavy wood and broke the door. The door was open.

◆

Sheherezade stopped.

'Well?' said the sultan. 'What happened next? What *was* behind the door?'

'Sir, there's light in the sky,' said Sheherezade. 'You're going to kill me now.'

'But you can't stop there. You have to finish the story.'

'Then please give me another day,' said Sheherezade.

The sultan was angry, but he said, 'All right, I'll give you one more day. But after that . . .'

The next night, Sheherezade started her story again.

◆

Behind the door, everything was very dark and quiet. Then Salem saw some stairs. He took a lamp and walked down the stairs. The stairs went down for a long way into the ground and came out into a cave. Salem walked through the cave and came to the sea.

He stood there and looked round him. Then he saw something in the sky. It got bigger and bigger. It was a very large bird. It came down and caught him by his clothes. Then it flew with him across the sea.

Salem was afraid, but then he slept. The bird flew all night.

Early next morning, Salem woke up and saw a beautiful beach below him. A lot of people waited on the beach. The bird flew down into the middle of the people.

The people were very friendly to Salem. They brought him a fine horse and helped him onto it. Then they took him through lovely gardens to a beautiful house. Inside the house, there was a lovely woman sitting on a chair.

When she saw Salem, she got up. 'You're here, my love! I'm very happy now,' she said.

She took Salem's hand and walked with him through the house and gardens.

'Everything here is mine,' she said. 'Stay with me and be my husband. Then this will be yours too.'

'I would like that,' answered Salem.

'But there is one thing,' said the woman. They went back to the first room and she showed Salem a door. 'Don't open that door,' she said, 'or you'll be unhappy every day of your life.'

Salem took the woman's hand. 'I don't want to open the door,' he said. 'I only want you.'

Salem married the beautiful woman, and they lived happily for many years. He wasn't interested in the door. But then he began to think about it more and more.

'I opened the first door, at the old man's house,' he thought, 'and I found this lovely place. When I open this door, perhaps I'll find a more wonderful place.'

One day, he couldn't wait. This time, he didn't have to break the door. He pushed it and it opened easily.

Everything was dark behind the door. After some minutes, Salem saw a large eye. Then he saw a large bird. It was the bird from the cave outside the first door.

The bird jumped into the room. Salem tried to run away but it was too late. The bird caught him by his clothes and pulled him outside. It flew up into the sky, and the house and garden got smaller and smaller. The bird started to fly over the sea, and Salem slept.

After a day and a night, Salem woke up. He was in the cave by the sea again. The bird wasn't there. Salem walked through the

She walked with him through the house and gardens.

cave and found some stairs. He walked slowly up the stairs and found a door. He went through the door and he was in his old house in the city again.

For many months, he tried to find a way back to the wonderful country. But nobody knew anything about it.

In the end, he understood. No ship could take him to that lovely country and his beautiful wife.

'Now I understand about the old men,' he thought. 'They were unhappy because they made the same journey. They found that wonderful place. Then they lost everything too.'

Salem lived in the house all his life. He dressed in black clothes and he cried every day. He never laughed again.

◆

'That was a very sad story,' said the sultan. 'But the world is a very sad place.' He too never laughed these days.

'But is the world really sad?' said Sheherezade. 'Everybody has to laugh sometimes. I can tell you a funny story about a great man – oh, but it's too late.'

'But I want to know,' said the sultan. 'I think I can give you another day. You will tell me the story tonight.'

So that night, Sheherezade told the story.

Chapter 3   Sultan Haroun Laughs

The great Sultan Haroun couldn't sleep. One night, he suddenly said to his vizir, 'The night is long. I want it to be shorter. What can I do?'

The sultan had a servant, Masrour. Masrour helped the sultan night and day. Now he began to laugh.

The sultan was angry. 'Why are you laughing?' he asked. 'Are you laughing because I can't sleep?'

'No, sir,' answered Masrour. 'I'm not laughing at you. I'm thinking about something funny. You see, yesterday I walked down to the River Tigris. There were a lot of people there. They stood round a big fat man. The fat man told funny stories and did funny things. Everybody laughed at him.'

'Well, go and find this fat man,' said the sultan. 'Bring him to me. I can't sleep. Perhaps I can laugh at him too.'

Masrour went to the fat man's house. The man's name was Abdurrazak. He was asleep and he didn't want to get up. But when he heard about Sultan Haroun, he dressed quickly and came outside.

'Let's go,' he said. 'Let's not be late for a great man.'

'Wait,' said Masrour. 'The sultan will laugh at you and give you a lot of money. But think. Who told him about you? It was me, Masrour. So you have to give me something too. When the sultan gives you your fee, one half is yours. Give the other half to me.'

Abdurrazak wasn't very happy about this, but in the end he said yes. Then Masrour took him to the sultan.

When Sultan Haroun saw Abdurrazak, he said, 'So people in the street laugh at you. But I'm a sultan. Will I laugh at you too?'

Abdurrazak began to say and do funny things. Masrour laughed and laughed. Then the vizir laughed. But the sultan didn't laugh. Abdurrazak was very surprised. Then he began to feel afraid.

'Stop!' said Haroun. 'You're a very stupid man and you aren't funny. So here's your fee. Masrour, hit this man hard ten times.'

So Masrour began to hit the unhappy Abdurrazak. One ... two ... three ... four ... five.

Then Abdurrazak cried, 'Stop, Masrour! That's one half of my fee. Now take your half.'

'What's this?' said the sultan. 'What do you mean – " one half of my fee"?'

Abdurrazak began to say and do funny things.

So Masrour told the sultan about Abdurrazak's fee – one half for Abdurrazak and the other half for Masrour.

When he finished, the sultan asked Masrour, 'Well, do you want your half of the fee?'

'No, sir,' answered Masrour. 'Abdurrazak can take the fee – my half and his half.'

'All right, then,' said the sultan. 'Abdurrazak will take Masrour's half. Masrour, hit him five more times.'

Masrour hit Abdurrazak five more times. After he finished, Abdurrazak wanted to run away. But the sultan said, 'Don't go, Abdurrazak. That was only the first half of your fee. Now you have to take the second half.'

Abdurrazak's face turned white. He was very afraid. What second half? What did the sultan mean?

The sultan turned to his vizir. 'This is the second half,' he said. 'My vizir will give you a hundred pieces of gold. Now, Abdurrazak, take your fee and go home.'

The sultan turned to look at Masrour. Masrour's face was very unhappy but it was also very funny. Now, and for the first time that night – the sultan laughed.

◆

'I liked that story,' said Sultan Shahriar. 'But it was very short. There's time for one more story.'

So Sheherezade began her next story.

Chapter 4   Faisal and the Barber

Faisal was a rich young man of Baghdad. He lived in a large house with many servants. But he didn't have a wife. He wasn't interested in love.

One day, Faisal went for a walk in the streets of the city. He saw a lot of young girls in front of him. He didn't want to meet them, so he turned into a small street. He looked up and saw a beautiful young girl at a window. From that minute, Faisal was in love.

Then a man on a horse came into the street. He had many servants with him. He stopped outside the girl's house and went inside.

'Is that her father?' Faisal thought.

He went home, but he couldn't eat or sleep. He thought about the girl. Who was she? He had to know.

An old woman worked in Faisal's house. She asked, 'What's wrong with you, sir? Are you ill?'

'No,' answered Faisal. 'But I'm in love.' He told the old woman about the girl at the window.

'I know that girl,' said the old woman. 'She's the daughter of a judge. Her father is a very important man.'

'How can I meet her?' asked Faisal.

'Listen,' said the old woman. 'I know the people in the girl's house. I'll speak to the girl about you. She'll listen to me.'

The old woman went to the house and spoke to the girl about Faisal. The girl listened. She was very interested.

'I would like to meet this young man,' she said. 'On Fridays, my father always goes out in the morning. Tell the young man. He can come and see me then. I'll speak to him.'

◆

When Friday came, Faisal was very excited. First he went to the baths. Then he sent a servant into the town for a barber.

Faisal wanted the barber to cut his hair. But the barber was very slow and talked about stupid things.

'Be quick!' said Faisal. 'I have to visit friends.'

'Friends!' said the barber. 'Oh, no! Now I remember. Some friends are visiting me today, but I forgot to buy food for them. What will they think of me?'

He looked up and saw a beautiful young girl at a window.

'Listen,' said Faisal, 'I have a lot of food in my house, but I'm going out. I don't want it, so you can take it. But finish your work and GO!'

'Thank you, thank you,' said the barber. 'But now what can I do for you? I know! I can come with you to your friends' house.'

'No, you can't,' said Faisal.

'Oh,' said the barber. Then he got very excited. 'Perhaps your friend is a woman? Yes! Perhaps things will be difficult for you? But, really, I can help you. I helped a lot of my friends in this way. Please let me come with you.'

Faisal didn't want to listen to the barber. 'Oh, all right,' he said. 'Take the food home to your friends. I'll wait for you here. Then you can come with me to my friends' house.'

But Faisal didn't wait for the barber. He didn't want the barber to come with him. When the barber left, he went to the girl's house. He was very late because of the barber. The old woman opened the door and took him upstairs to a fine room. There he sat and waited for the girl.

But the barber didn't go home. He paid a man, and the man took the food back to his house. Then he followed Faisal to the girl's house. When Faisal went into the house, the barber waited outside in the street.

Suddenly, he saw the judge, the girl's father. The judge came down the street and went into the house.

Inside, the judge found a servant. The servant had the judge's money in his hand, so the judge began to hit the man hard.

Outside in the street, the barber heard the man's cries. 'It's my friend, Faisal,' he thought. 'The judge is killing him.' He ran to the door and began to shout. 'Help! Help!' he cried. 'The judge is killing my friend!'

Many people heard the barber and came out of their houses. They stood round the judge's door and began to cry, 'Help! Help! The judge is killing this man's friend!'

From inside the house, the judge heard the noise and opened the door. When he saw the angry people, he was surprised and a little afraid.

Then the barber said to him, 'Where's my friend?'

'Yes, where's his friend?' asked the people. They were very excited.

'I don't understand,' said the judge. 'Who is this man's friend? Why is he in my house?'

'You bad old man!' shouted the barber. 'My friend loves your daughter, and she loves him! You know that very well. So you killed him.'

'Good people,' said the judge, 'my house is open to everybody. But I'm telling you, this man's friend isn't inside. Come and look.'

The barber ran into the house and the people followed him. Faisal heard the noise and was very afraid. He found a large box and climbed into it. Then the barber came in.

'There you are, my friend!' he said. 'You'll be all right now. I'm here and I'm going to help you.'

He closed the box and began to carry it downstairs. There were many people on the stairs and he pushed them out of his way.

But Faisal was very angry with the barber.

'Go away, you stupid man!' he shouted. 'I don't want your help.' He began to kick the box hard from the inside.

The barber fell down the stairs and the box fell out of his arms onto the floor. Faisal climbed out. His arm hurt and his face was black and blue. He pushed his way through the people and ran home quickly. He had to get away from the barber. But the barber followed him and shouted, 'Wait for me, my friend! I only want to help you!'

◆

Shahriar laughed and laughed. In the next room, the vizir stopped his work and listened. He was very surprised.

15

'Why is the sultan laughing?' he thought. 'And what is Sheherezade doing? Why isn't she dead?'

The next night, Sheherezade began a new story.

Chapter 5   The Boy Judge

Ali had a cake shop in the city of Baghdad. He wasn't rich but he was a good man. He worked hard.

Ali had a jar under the floor of his shop. Every week, he put a small piece of gold into this jar. This money was for him when he was old and ill.

When Ali was fifty years old, he took out the jar. There were more than a thousand gold pieces inside.

'I have a lot of money now,' he thought. 'I would like to see the world before I die.'

So Ali sold his shop. But there was one problem – the jar of gold. He couldn't take it with him on the journey.

Then he had an idea. He bought some olives and put them in the jar on top of the gold. Then Ali closed the jar and took it to his friend, Husein. Husein also had a shop.

'Please can I leave this jar of olives with you?' he asked.

'Of course, my friend,' said Husein. 'Leave the jar of olives with me. Put it here in my shop.'

Ali was away for a long time. He went to Egypt and then Syria.

One day, when Ali was in Syria, Husein's wife wanted some olives. But the shop in their street was shut.

'There are some olives in my shop,' said Husein. 'Do you remember? Ali left a jar of olives with me, but he never came back. Perhaps he's dead. So we can eat his olives.'

Husein went to his shop and opened the jar of olives. But the olives at the top were very old and dry. He put his hand down into the jar and pulled out – not an olive, but a piece of gold.

'Please can I leave this jar of olives with you?'

Then he pulled out more pieces of gold.

Husein was very surprised. He thought for a long time. In the end, he took the olives out of the jar and threw them away. Then he took the gold out of the jar and put it under the floor of his shop. To his wife, he said only, 'We can't use those olives. They were too old and dry.'

Next, he bought new olives. He put them in the jar and closed it.

'Perhaps Ali will come back,' he thought. 'He gave me a jar of olives. So I'll give him back a jar of olives.'

Some weeks later, Ali came back to Baghdad after seven years. He went to Husein and asked for his jar of olives.

'Olives?' said Husein. 'What olives?'

'I left a jar of olives with you. You put it in your shop.'

'Oh, yes,' said Husein. 'I'm sorry, I forgot. Seven years is a long time. Let's go to my shop and I'll give it to you.'

When Ali saw the jar of olives, he felt very happy.

'Thank you, my friend,' said Ali. 'Now I want to give you something.'

Ali put his hand in the jar and pulled out – not gold pieces, but olives. He did this again and again. In the end he said, 'Where's my gold? What happened to my gold?'

'Gold? What gold?' asked Husein.

'I had some gold in this jar.'

'My friend, you left a jar of olives with me. You said nothing about a jar of gold.'

'There was gold in the jar under the olives,' said Ali. 'Please give it back to me.'

'I know nothing about any gold,' answered Husein.

They talked about this for some time. Then Ali said, 'Let's go to the judge. He'll help me, you'll see.'

Ali and Husein went to the judge.

The judge asked Ali, 'Did anybody see the gold in the jar?'

'No,' answered Ali.

'Did you tell anybody about the gold in the jar?'

'No.'

'What did you say to Husein? What was in the jar?'

'Olives.'

'Ali,' said the judge. 'You're an old man. You don't remember things very well. Nobody saw the gold. You told nobody about it. So perhaps there *was* no gold in the jar.'

Ali was very angry with the judge, so he wrote a letter to the sultan. The sultan was very interested in Ali's story. Now everybody in Baghdad knew about the jar of olives. But who was right – Ali or Husein?

The sultan said to his vizir, 'Let's walk in the streets tonight and listen to people. What are they saying about Ali and Husein?'

That night, the sultan and his vizir saw some children in the street. The children spoke the names of Ali and Husein.

'Those children are playing a game,' said the vizir. 'One boy is Ali and one is Husein. Another boy is playing the judge.'

The sultan listened to the boy judge and said, 'That boy is very clever. He asks very good questions. Bring him to me tomorrow morning. Bring Ali and Husein, the judge, the jar of olives and two olive sellers too.'

The next day, these people came to the sultan.

'Come, boy,' the sultan said. 'Sit by me. Yesterday you judged Ali and Husein in play. Now you will really do it. And you,' he said to the judge, 'listen to this boy and learn from him. He knows about right and wrong, good men and thieves.'

The boy was very afraid, but he said, 'Bring me the jar of olives. Now,' he said to Ali, 'did you give this jar to Husein?'

'Yes,' answered Ali.

'Did Ali give this jar to you?' he asked Husein.

'Yes,' answered Husein.

The boy pulled out some olives from the jar and ate them. Then he said to Husein, 'These olives are good. Did you eat any?'

'No,' said Husein. 'I didn't open the jar when Ali was away from Baghdad.'

The boy gave some olives to the two olive sellers. 'Try these olives,' he said. 'They're seven years old but they're very good.'

'Seven years old!' cried the olive sellers. 'These olives aren't seven years old. No olive is good after three years. It loses its colour. These olives are *this* year's olives.'

'But Husein says these olives were in the jar for seven years,' said the boy judge.

Everybody looked at Husein. Husein's face turned white.

'I took the gold,' he said. 'I'm sorry, Ali.'

So Husein lost his good name. Ali had his gold again, but lost a friend. And the boy stayed with the sultan and later was a famous judge.

◆

'There aren't many good judges,' said Shahriar.

'I know another story about a judge,' said Sheherezade. 'A judge and a dwarf. It's very funny. But there's no time.'

'Yes, there's time. I'll give you another night.'

So the next night, Sheherezade started a new story.

Chapter 6   The Dwarf of Basra

A man lived in the city of Basra and sold fish. One night, the fish seller met a dwarf in the street. The fish seller liked funny stories and the dwarf knew a lot of good stories. So the fish seller invited him to his house for dinner.

'My wife is cooking a big fish tonight,' he said. 'Come and eat it with us.'

The dwarf was hungry and the fish was good. The fish seller's wife gave him more and more food.

The dwarf was hungry and the fish was good.

'You're only a little man,' she said. 'You have to eat a lot of food. Then you'll be big.'

Her husband laughed and hit the dwarf on the back. He did this in a friendly way, but the dwarf had a lot of food in his mouth. A large piece of fish went down the wrong way inside him.

The dwarf felt very ill. He couldn't speak and his face turned first red, then blue. He fell onto the floor and didn't move. The fish seller was afraid.

'The dwarf is dead,' he thought. 'I don't want a dead man in my house. It was an accident, but there will be questions. The people will take me to the judge. What will the judge say? What will happen to me?'

'Let's get the dwarf out of our house,' said his wife.

The fish seller thought. Then he carried the dwarf outside. A doctor lived across the road on the first floor. The fish seller climbed the doctor's stairs and sat the dwarf down outside his door. Then he made a loud noise and ran away.

The doctor opened his door quickly. But when he did this, the door hit the dwarf hard. The dwarf fell down to the bottom of the stairs. The doctor ran downstairs after him, but the dwarf didn't move.

'This little man is dead!' he said. 'It was an accident, but what will everybody say? "He's a doctor but he kills people." Nobody will come to me again. What am I going to do?'

Then he had an idea. He looked up and down the street. It was late, and nobody was outside. An old bird seller lived in the next house.

'I know,' thought the doctor. 'I'll throw the dwarf over the wall into the old bird seller's garden. Then the dwarf will be his problem, not mine.'

The dwarf went over the wall easily and came down near the birds. The birds started to make a loud noise. From inside the house, the old bird seller heard the noise.

'Somebody is hurting my birds,' he thought. He ran outside

and saw the dwarf on the ground near the birds. He started to hit him hard on the head. 'Thief! What are you doing with my birds?' he shouted. 'Tell me!'

But the dwarf didn't speak. He didn't move. Then the old bird seller was afraid and looked at the dwarf again.

'This little man is dead,' he thought. 'I hit him, but I didn't want to kill him. What will the judge say?'

Then he had an idea. He looked out of his garden. Nobody was outside. He carried the dwarf down the street to a big house. A very rich man lived in that house. He put the dwarf in front of the rich man's door. Then he ran home.

The rich man was out for the evening with friends. When he came home, he found the dwarf in front of his door.

'Wake up!' he shouted angrily. 'You can't sleep here!'

He began to kick the dwarf hard. The dwarf didn't wake up, but other people in the street heard him. One man came out of his house, and said, 'Stop! Stop! You'll kill that little man!'

The rich man stopped and looked down at the dwarf. But the dwarf didn't move.

'You see?' said the other man. 'Now he's dead.'

People looked out of their windows and shouted, 'He killed the dwarf! Let's take him to the judge!'

They took the rich man and the dwarf to the judge. It was the middle of the night and the judge was asleep. But he woke up and came outside. He looked at the dwarf and listened to the people.

The judge said to the rich man, 'You killed him. So now you have to die.'

The bird seller heard the judge's words. 'Please, sir', he said. This man didn't kill the dwarf. I did it. I hit him on the head. I didn't want to kill him, but he died. I left him by this man's door.'

'All right,' said the judge. 'So *you* have to die.'

When he heard this, the doctor thought, 'I don't like this old bird seller. But he can't die. I did it – not him.'

'Wait!' said the doctor. The old man didn't kill the dwarf. I killed him. I opened my door too quickly and pushed the dwarf down the stairs. Then I threw him into the old bird seller's garden.'

'When will we get to the end of this?' asked the judge. 'So *you* have to die.'

'No, no,' said the fish seller. '*I* killed the dwarf. It was an accident but I was afraid. I put him in front of the doctor's door. Some food went down the wrong way inside him and I hit him. I'll show you.'

The fish seller hit the dwarf on the back. But when he did this, a large piece of fish jumped out of the dwarf's mouth. The dwarf opened his eyes. He wasn't dead!

'What happened?' he said. 'Where am I?'

Then the judge spoke for the last time.

'The dwarf isn't dead,' he said, 'so nobody has to die. But you kicked and hit this little man. Each man will pay him fifty gold pieces. Now go home, and be kinder in future.'

◆

Sheherezade's next story was long and she told it for two nights. The sultan couldn't kill her. He had to hear the end of the story first.

Chapter 7   Ali Baba and the Forty Thieves

Kasim and Ali Baba were brothers. Kasim was rich with a shop, a fine house and a lovely garden. Ali Baba had very little money. He was a woodcutter with only two donkeys and a very small house. So the two brothers didn't often meet.

One day, Ali Baba wanted to cut wood. He took his two donkeys and walked a long way. He came to a mountain. There were a lot of good trees at the bottom of the mountain. But suddenly he heard the sound of horses. To Ali Baba, the sound meant only one thing – thieves! Quickly, he pushed his donkeys away and climbed a tree.

Ali Baba was right. They *were* thieves – forty thieves. They stopped near Ali Baba's tree and got down from their horses. Ali Baba was very afraid, but the thieves didn't see him.

The first thief went to the mountain. He stood in front of it and said very quietly, 'Open, Sesame!' Then the wall of the mountain opened and there was a large cave.

The thieves carried bags into the cave and the mountain closed behind them. Then they came out again and got on their horses. They went away through the trees.

Ali Baba was very surprised. When everything was quiet, he came down from his tree. He went to the mountain. He stood in front of it and said, 'Open, Sesame!'

The wall of the mountain opened and Ali Baba went into the cave. It was very dark inside. He couldn't see anything for a short time. Then he saw a lot of gold and other beautiful things.

Ali Baba found his donkeys. He put the gold in two bags and put firewood on the top. Then he went home.

It was very late when Ali Baba arrived home. He carried the bags into his house and showed the gold to his wife. She was very surprised and happy.

The next day, Ali Baba's wife met Kasim's wife in the town. Kasim's wife liked to know everything.

'Why are you happy today?' she asked.

'Something happened to Ali Baba yesterday,' answered his wife. 'It's very exciting. Now we're going to be rich.'

Kasim's wife went home and told her husband about Ali Baba. Kasim went to Ali Baba's house.

'Brother, my wife says you're going to be rich,' he said. 'Please tell me. How did it happen?'

Ali Baba said nothing, but Kasim asked again and again. In the

Then he saw a lot of gold and other beautiful things.

end, Ali Baba told his brother about the cave in the mountain.

Next morning, Kasim left home early and took twenty donkeys with him. He found the mountain and opened the cave. Then he went inside and the mountain closed behind him.

Kasim could think only of gold. He carried twenty bags of gold to the mouth of the cave. He wanted to open the cave again, but he couldn't remember the right words.

'Open, mountain!' he said. Then, 'Open, cave!' He tried a hundred ways. But the mountain didn't move.

Suddenly the forty thieves came back and saw the donkeys outside the cave. They opened the cave and ran inside. They found Kasim inside and they killed him with their knives.

'Let's cut this dead man into pieces,' they said. 'Perhaps other people know about this place too. When they see the pieces, they'll be afraid.'

They cut Kasim into four pieces and left the pieces inside the cave. Then they took his twenty donkeys and went away.

Night came, but Kasim didn't come home. His wife went to Ali Baba. 'Please, go and look for my husband,' she said.

So Ali Baba took his two donkeys and walked all night. In the morning, he came to the mountain. 'Open, Sesame!' he said, and the cave opened.

He saw the four pieces of his brother on the ground.

'The forty thieves did this,' he thought. 'Where are they now? Perhaps they'll come back. I have to be quick.' He put the four pieces of Kasim into a bag and went home.

Ali Baba didn't want people to ask questions about Kasim: 'Why is Kasim dead?' 'Who killed him?' 'Where?' 'How?' He didn't want everybody to know about the cave.

Kasim had a very clever servant girl, Marjana. Marjana always knew the answer to a problem. She went to a doctor in the town. 'Please, sir,' she said to the doctor. 'Kasim is very ill. Please give me something for him.'

In this way, the story quickly went round the town: Kasim was very ill. The next day, Marjana went to the doctor again. Later that day, Kasim's wife and Marjana began to cry loudly. People in the houses near Kasim's house heard them.

'Listen,' people said. 'Kasim's wife and servant are crying. Kasim was very ill and now he's dead.'

'Now everybody knows Kasim is dead,' said Ali Baba. 'But he's in four pieces. We can't put him into the ground. People will see him and ask questions: "Why is Kasim in four pieces?" "Who cut him into pieces?" "Where?"'

Again, Marjana had an idea. In the town, there was an old shoemaker. His eyes were very bad and he couldn't see anything. But he was very good at his work.

Marjana went to his house and gave the old man some gold. 'Come with me, and I'll give you more gold,' she said. 'I have four pieces of something. I want you to make the four pieces into one piece.'

She gave him the four pieces of Kasim. The old man worked hard all night. In the morning, Kasim was in one piece again, and they put him into the ground.

Ali Baba and his wife and children moved into Kasim's house with Kasim's wife and Marjana. They lived happily for a time. But the story didn't end there. Other people weren't very happy – the forty thieves.

Chapter 8 The End of the Forty Thieves

When the thieves came back to the cave, they were very surprised. Where were the four pieces of the dead man?

'Another person knows about our cave,' they thought. 'Perhaps the dead man had friends. But who *was* the dead man? We killed him before we could ask him.'

'I have an idea,' said one thief. 'I'll go into the town and ask some questions. Perhaps somebody will remember a dead man in four pieces.'

The thief went into the town. He asked a lot of questions but he didn't learn anything. Then he came to the shop of the old shoemaker. He watched the old man at work.

'Your work is very good, old man,' said the thief.

'Yes,' said the shoemaker. 'I can make everything. Last week, I made four pieces of a dead man into one piece.'

'Really?' said the thief. 'That's very interesting. Who was this dead man? Where did he live?'

'I don't know,' answered the shoemaker. 'A girl came here and took me to a house. I did my work there.'

'Take this gold,' said the thief. 'Can you remember the way to the house?'

The old shoemaker took the thief through the streets and stopped outside Kasim's door. 'This was the house,' he said.

The thief took the old man home. Then he went back to the other thirty-nine thieves and told them his story.

One evening some weeks later, a seller of oil came to the door of Kasim's house. He had twenty donkeys with him. Each donkey carried two big oil jars. The oil seller said to Ali Baba, 'Sir, I'm going to sell these jars of oil tomorrow. Please can I leave them outside your house tonight?'

'Bring in your donkeys and your jars,' said Ali Baba. 'You can eat with us and stay here for the night.'

The oil seller brought in his donkeys and jars. Then Ali Baba took him inside. Marjana was in the kitchen. She started to cook the dinner but the oil in her lamp went out.

'I know,' she thought. 'There's a lot of oil in the jars outside. I can take a little for my lamp.'

She went outside to the jars. When she got to the first jar, a man asked from inside the jar, 'Is it time?'

A man asked from inside the jar, 'Is it time?'

Marjana was very surprised but she thought quickly. She answered, 'No, it isn't time.'

Then she went to every jar. From each jar, she heard the same question and gave the same answer. Only the last jar really had oil in it.

Something was very wrong.

'The men in these jars are thirty-nine thieves,' Marjana thought. 'The oil seller is a thief too. They are going to kill Ali Baba and his family. I have to do something.'

She carried the oil from the last jar into the kitchen and put it over the fire. When the oil was very hot, she went outside and put some hot oil into every jar.

In this way, she killed thirty-nine of the forty thieves. But the last thief, the most dangerous, was upstairs with Ali Baba and his family.

Later that night, Ali Baba and his family were asleep in bed. But Marjana was in her kitchen. She waited for the thief.

He came downstairs and went outside. Marjana watched him. He went to the first jar and said, 'It's time.' But there was no answer from the jar.

The thief looked inside and saw a dead man. He was very surprised and afraid. He ran from jar to jar and found the same thing in every jar. Then he came to the last jar. There was nothing in it.

Marjana began to make a loud noise from the kitchen. The thief was afraid and climbed into the jar. Then Marjana carried more hot oil to the jar and put it on top of the thief inside. Now he was dead too.

In the morning, Marjana told Ali Baba everything.

'Thank you very much, Marjana,' said Ali Baba. 'You are a very clever girl. Will you marry my son?'

So Marjana lived happily with the family for many years.

◆

At the end of the story, Shahriar said to Sheherezade, 'Marjana was really very clever. Some girls make clever plans, and then men will do everything for them. Not you, I hope.'

'Oh no, sir,' answered Sheherezade. 'I only want to make you happy.'

'Then tell me a new story tonight,' said Shahriar.

Chapter 9   The Thief and the Donkey

Two thieves stood in a busy street in the city. One of them looked at the people and said, 'Look at those people! They're very stupid. I can take something from everybody.'

'You think you can do that,' said the other thief. 'You talk about it, but can you really do it? I don't think people are really stupid. Look at that man with the donkey over there. Can you take his donkey from him?'

'Yes,' said the first thief. 'With a little help from you, I can take his donkey from him and he will say "thank you" to me for it. Come with me and I'll show you.'

The two thieves followed the man down the street. The man pulled the donkey behind him. The first thief went behind the donkey and changed places with it. At the same time, the second thief took the donkey away.

So the man pulled a person, not his donkey, but he didn't know this. The thief walked behind the man for a little way but suddenly he stopped. The man pulled and pulled. The thief didn't move. So the man turned round. He was very surprised when he saw the thief.

'Who are you?' he cried. 'And where's my donkey?'

'Oh, sir, don't ask me,' answered the thief. 'I *was* your donkey, but now I'm a man again. Listen to my sad story.

'I lived with my mother, a good old woman. But I wasn't

a good son. She wanted me to live a better life, but I didn't listen to her.

'One night, I came home very late. My mother was angry with me. Then I got angry too and started to hit her. She shouted, "Will you never change, my son? You are as stupid as a donkey. Perhaps one day you'll really change into a donkey."'

'Suddenly I began to feel different. My ears got longer and my arms changed into legs. When I tried to speak, I could only make donkey noises.'

'So you really changed into a donkey!' said the man.

'Yes. I ran outside into the street. The next morning, a man caught me. He took me into the town and sold me. He sold me to you, sir.

'Then a very bad time began for me. Sometimes you hit me and didn't give me much food. Sometimes you put very heavy things on my back.

'Then today, I walked down this street and I saw my old mother. When she saw me, she cried. She said, "You're a nice little donkey! I had a son, but he changed into a donkey. Perhaps one day he'll change into a man again." And suddenly I was a man again.'

When he heard this, the man said, 'Oh, my dear brother, I'm very sorry. I know I was often unkind to you. But I didn't know you were really a man. I thought you were only a donkey. Here, take this money. Buy food and drink and go home again to your old mother.'

The thief took the money and went away. He was very happy with his morning's work.

When the man arrived home, his wife asked, 'Where's your donkey?'

'We have no donkey,' answered the man, and he told his wife the thief's story.

'You were right when you gave money to that man,' said the wife. 'But you can't do your work without a donkey. Tomorrow, go into the town and buy a new one.'

My ears got longer and my arms changed into legs.

The next day, the man went into the town. He saw a donkey in the street. He went to it and looked at it carefully. Then he was very surprised.

'This is my old donkey,' he thought.

He spoke quietly into the donkey's ear and said, 'So you hit your old mother again and she changed you back into a donkey. Well, I'll never buy you again!'

◆

'That was a very funny story,' said the sultan. 'But it's only the middle of the night. I know you have a new story for me.'

He was right. Sheherezade had another story.

Chapter 10   Aladdin and the Lamp

Aladdin lived with his mother in a great city. They had very little money. Aladdin's father was dead and his mother made clothes for rich people. Aladdin helped her in her work.

One day, a man stopped Aladdin in the street. This man wore very fine clothes.

'Hello, Aladdin,' he said. 'I'm your uncle – your father's brother. I came here from Morocco. I wanted to see him but he's dead. So I'd really like to help you. Perhaps I can buy you a shop.'

Aladdin was very surprised. He didn't know his father had a brother. They walked round the city, then the man said, 'It's a nice day. Let's go outside the city.'

They walked for a long time, and Aladdin got very tired. Then his uncle stopped and hit the ground three times. There was a great noise and the ground opened.

Aladdin saw some dark stairs. They went down into the ground for a long way. Aladdin didn't like these stairs, but his uncle pushed him down them.

'Listen, boy', he said. 'At the bottom of the stairs there's a cave. Go through the cave and you'll come to a garden of fruit trees. You'll see a dirty old lamp under a tree. Bring that lamp to me. Now go! Be quick!'

Aladdin was afraid of the stairs but he was more afraid of his uncle. So he went down the stairs to the cave. He walked through the garden and found the lamp. He put it inside his shirt. Then he started to take some fruit from the trees. The fruit was pieces of gold! He put the gold inside his shirt too.

His uncle waited at the top of the stairs.

'Give me the lamp before you climb out. Then I'll help you,' said his uncle.

But Aladdin didn't like this idea. 'No,' he answered. 'Help me first, then I'll give you the lamp.'

Aladdin's uncle got very angry. He tried to take the lamp from Aladdin.

Suddenly there was a loud noise and everything went black. The ground closed over Aladdin.

Aladdin's uncle wasn't really his uncle. He was a magician. He wanted the lamp in the cave but the place was dangerous. So he used Aladdin. But now he couldn't get the lamp.

'Stupid boy!' he said, and he went back angrily to Morocco.

It was very dark in the cave. Aladdin couldn't get out. He stayed in the cave for two days and two nights.

'Why did my uncle want this dirty old lamp?' he thought. He moved his hands over the lamp. Suddenly, there was a loud noise and a large genie stood in front of him.

'I'm the genie of the lamp,' he said. 'What can I do for you, sir?'

Aladdin was surprised but he only wanted one thing. 'I want to go home,' he said.

The next minute, he was at home with his mother. He told her his story. His mother was very interested. 'Let's ask this genie for more things,' she said.

'I'm the genie of the lamp,' he said.

So Aladdin called the genie and the genie came.

'I'm very hungry,' said Aladdin. 'Bring my dinner.'

The genie brought wonderful food on gold plates. Then Aladdin and his mother asked for new clothes and other things. The genie brought everything.

For a time, Aladdin was happy. Then, one day, he saw the sultan's beautiful daughter in a garden. From that minute, he was in love with her and wanted to marry her.

Aladdin dressed in fine clothes and went to see the sultan. He took forty servants with him. Each servant carried a gold box with many beautiful things inside. The sultan couldn't say no to Aladdin.

'This man is very rich,' he thought. 'He'll be a good husband for my daughter.'

So Aladdin married the sultan's daughter. The genie brought them a lovely house and they lived there happily.

But one person wasn't happy – the magician in Morocco. He couldn't stop thinking about the lamp. Was it under the ground with that stupid boy? Or did the boy get out of the cave? Were the boy and the lamp somewhere in the city? He had to know the answers to these questions. So he came back to Aladdin's city.

The magician put on old clothes and bought some new lamps. Then he went round the streets of the city and cried, 'New lamps for old lamps! New lamps for old lamps!'

People laughed at him and brought their old lamps to him. 'This lamp seller is stupid,' they thought.

The magician changed their old lamps for new ones. Then he stopped outside Aladdin's house. Aladdin was out, but his wife sat at a window. She saw the magician and said to a servant girl, 'There's a dirty old lamp in my husband's room. Give it to that man.'

When the magician had the lamp in his hands, he called the genie. The genie came and said, 'Sir, what can I do for you?'

'Take me, this house and everything in it to Morocco.'

A big black cloud came down over the house. When the cloud went away again, Aladdin's house wasn't there.

When Aladdin came home, he cried, 'This is that magician's work. What am I going to do?'

He went to Morocco and looked for his house. After a long time, he found it. His wife was inside. When she saw Aladdin, she put her arms round him.

'You're here, my love! I'm very happy now,' she cried. 'The magician comes to see me every night. He wants me to forget you and marry him.'

'And my lamp?' asked Aladdin. 'Where is it?'

'He carries it with him.'

'I have to get that lamp,' said Aladdin. 'You'll have to help me. Put something in the magician's drink tonight.'

That night, Aladdin waited in the next room. His wife put something in the magician's drink and he slept. Then Aladdin cut off his head.

Aladdin took the lamp and called the genie.

'Sir, what can I do for you?' the genie asked.

'Take this house and everything in it back to my city.'

Aladdin and his wife flew back home and lived happily for many years. But the lamp always stayed with Aladdin.

◆

'How many stories do you know?' Shahriar asked.

'I know stories for a thousand and one nights. And when I finish those stories, I'll think of new ones.'

'Then I can never cut off your head. But I don't want to kill you. I love you, Sheherezade.'

So Sheherezade won the sultan's love with her stories. She loved him too, and they were very happy.

ACTIVITIES

Chapters 1–4

Before you read

1 Read the Introduction. Do you know these stories in your language? Do you know the names Ali Baba and Aladdin? What do you know about them?

2 Look at the Word List at the back of the book. Find new words in your dictionary.

    a Seven of these words are for people. Which words?

    b Which five things can you find in a shop?

While you read

3 Which is the right word?

    a Sultan Shahriar cuts off his *vizir's / wife's* head.

    b Sheherezade *wants / doesn't want* to marry the sultan.

    c Sheherezade wants her *father / sister* to sleep in the room with her and the sultan.

    d An hour *before / after* morning comes, Dunyazade speaks to her sister.

4 When do these happen in the story 'Behind the Door'? Number the sentences, 1–5.

    a Salem opens the door in the old man's room. .....

    b An old man takes Salem to a beautiful house. .....

    c Salem's father leaves him a lot of money and houses. .....

    d The eleven old men in the house die. .....

    e Salem loses his money and works in the streets. .....

5 Are these sentences right (✓) or wrong (✗)?

    a In the morning, the sultan wants to cut off Sheherezade's head. .....

    b A very big bird carries Salem across the sea. .....

    c Salem doesn't open the door in his new house. .....

    d When Salem goes back to his old house, he is very happy. .....

41

6 Which of the people in the story 'Sultan Haroun Laughs':

   a can't sleep? ....

   b tells the sultan about a funny man? ....

   c doesn't laugh at Abdurrazak? ....

   d hits Abdurrazak ten times? ....

   e gives Abdurrazak 100 gold pieces? ....

7 Finish these sentences about 'Faisal and the Barber'. Write one word.

   a Faisal sees a girl at a .... and falls in love with her.

   b The girl's father is a ....

   c The .... follows Faisal to the girl's house.

   d Inside the house, the judge hits one of his ....

   e Faisal is afraid and he climbs into a ....

   f At the end of this story, the sultan ....

After you read

8 Who says these words? Why are they important in the story?

   a 'Please tell me a story.'

   b 'But you can't stop there.'

   c 'I can tell you a funny story … oh, but it's too late.'

9 Discuss these questions.

   a Why was the vizier unhappy when his daughter wanted to marry the sultan? Why is he surprised after the third night?

   b In 'Behind the Door', Salem opens two doors. Is he clever or stupid? Why?

   c In 'Sultan Haroun Laughs', Masrour tries to be clever. What does he get at the end? What does Abdurrazak get? Is this a good end to the story? Why (not)?

   d In 'Faisal and the Barber', is the barber a good friend to Faisal? Why (not)?

Chapters 5–7

Before you read

10 The next three stories are about thieves and judges. These old stories teach a lesson to their readers. Do you know any stories about thieves or judges? Tell one to the class. What is the lesson?

While you read

11 Are these sentences about 'The Boy Judge' right (✓) or wrong (✗)?

    a When he is fifty, Ali put his gold in a jar under
       some olives.   .....

    b He leaves the jar with his friend, Husein.   .....

    c Husein finds the gold.   .....

    d Ali doesn't come back for seven months.   .....

    e When Ali comes back, the gold is in the jar.   .....

    f The judge thinks that Husein took the gold.   .....

    g The boy knows that the olives in the jar are new.   .....

12 Find the right end to these sentences about 'The Dwarf of Basra'.

    a The fish seller puts the dwarf   outside a rich man's house.

    b The doctor puts the dwarf   outside the doctor's house.

    c The bird seller puts the dwarf   in the bird seller's garden.

13 Finish these sentences with names from 'Ali Baba and the Forty Thieves'.

    a There are two brothers but only .... is rich.

    b .... hears the thieves and climbs a tree.

    c .... takes two bags of gold from the cave.

    d Ali Baba's wife tells ....'s wife about the cave.

    e .... goes to the cave with twenty donkeys.

    f The thieves kill .... and cut him into pieces.

    g .... takes the four pieces of Kasim to a shoemaker.

After you read

14 Answer these questions.

    a Why is the boy a clever judge?

    b Why does the fish seller invite the dwarf to his home?

    c How does Kasim know about the gold in the cave?

    d Why can't Kasim get out of the cave?

15 Work with another student. Have this conversation.

    Student A: You are Kasim's wife. You meet Ali Baba's wife in the
                  town. She is happy and excited. Ask her why.

    Student B: You are Ali Baba's wife. Tell Kasim's wife something
                  – but not everything.

Chapters 8–10

Before you read

16 Ali Baba's family are now rich and Kasim is in the ground. What will the forty thieves think when they go back to the cave? What will they do?

While you read

17 Finish these sentences about 'The End of the Forty Thieves'.

a The thieves are surprised because ....

....

b Marjana is surprised because ....

....

c The last thief is surprised because ....

....

18 In 'The Thief and the Donkey', when do these happen? Number the sentences, 1–5.

a The thief says that he was the man's donkey.   .....

b The man finds his donkey again.   .....

c The man thinks that the thief hit his mother again.   .....

d The two thieves want to take the man's donkey.   .....

e The man gives the thief money.   .....

19 Write answers to the questions about 'Aladdin and the Lamp'. Who or what:

a takes Aladdin outside the city?   ....

b goes down into a garden under the ground?   ....

c comes out of the old lamp?   ....

d does Aladdin fall in love with?   ....

e gives people new lamps for old lamps?   ....

f puts something in the magician's drink?   ....

After you read

20 Work with another student. Have this conversation.

    Student A: You are the man in 'The Thief and the Donkey'. Today you have a new donkey. Answer your friend's questions.

    Student B: Your friend (from 'The Thief and the Donkey') has a new donkey. Ask him about his old donkey. What do you think of his story? Tell him.

21 Answer these questions.

    a Why doesn't the magician go into the cave and get the lamp?

    b Why is the sultan happy when Aladdin wants to marry his daughter?

    c How does Aladdin get the lamp from the magician?

    d Would you like a lamp with a genie in it? What would you like from him?

Writing

22 You are Sheherezade. Tomorrow you are going to marry the sultan, but you don't want to die. Write a letter to your father, the vizir. Tell him about your plan.

23 At the end of 'Behind the Door', Salem is unhappy and never laughs again. You are Salem. Write your story. It will be a lesson for other young men.

24 You are Faisal in 'Faisal and the Barber'. Write a letter to the judge. Say sorry. Tell him about the stupid barber. Say that you would like to meet his daughter.

25 You are Husein in 'The Boy Judge'. Ali now has his gold again. People call you a thief. Write a letter to Ali. Say you are sorry. Say that you want to be his friend again.

26 You work for a newspaper in Basra. You find the dwarf in hospital. He is ill but rich. Write about his story for your newspaper. Call the story, 'The "Dead" Dwarf'.

27 You are Ali Baba's wife. You have very little money and live in a small house. But today Ali Baba came home with some gold and a very strange story about a cave in the mountains. Write a letter to your mother. Tell her everything.

28 In these stories some people are clever and good, and some people are bad or stupid. Write about one clever person and one stupid person from the stories. What did they do?

29 Write a story. Begin:

One day I found an old lamp in a shop. I took it home and a genie came out of it.

The genie said, 'What can I do for you? I can do anything!'

WORD LIST *with example sentences*

barber (n) The *barber* cut my hair too short.

cave (n) The animals live in cold, dark *caves*.

cloud (n) There were dark *clouds* in the sky and then it rained.

donkey (n) A horse is too big. I'm going to go on a *donkey*.

dwarf (n) She told the children the story of Snow White and the Seven *Dwarves*.

fee (n) Have you got the money for your university *fees*?

genie (n) In the story, the *genie* lives in a bottle.

gold (n/adj) Somebody found *gold* here and now a lot of people are coming.

jar (n) There is some money in a *jar* in the kitchen cupboard.

judge (n) It was an accident! Please tell the *judge*.

lamp (n) The lights aren't working. Have you got a *lamp*?

magician (n) The *magician* put his hand behind her ear and pulled out an egg.

oil (n) Shall I cook this fish in *oil*?

olive (n) We have twenty *olive* trees in our garden in Spain.

piece (n) I'll eat that small *piece* of meat in a sandwich.

servant (n) Forty visitors are coming this weekend, so the *servants* will have to do a lot of cooking.

sultan (n) He was the *sultan*, so his people listened to him.

surprised (adj) I didn't know about the party. I was very *surprised*.

tale (n) He gave me a book of old Chinese *tales*.

thief (n) *Thieves* took the computers from our offices.

Treasure Island
Robert Louis Stevenson

A young boy, Jim Hawkins, lives quietly by the sea with his mother and father. One day, Billy Bones comes to live with them and from that day everything is different. Jim meets Long John Silver, a man with one leg, and Jim and Long John Silver go far across the sea in a ship called the *Hispaniola* to Treasure Island.

The Mummy

"Imhotep is half-dead and will be half-dead for all time."

The Mummy is an exciting movie. Imhotep dies in Ancient Egypt. 3,700 years later Rick O'Connell finds him. Imhotep is very dangerous. Can O'Connell send him back to the dead?

The Last of the Mohicans
James Fenimore Cooper

Uncas is the last of the Mohican Indians. He is with his father and Hawkeye when they meet Heyward. Heyward is taking the two young daughters of a British colonel to their father. But a Huron Indian who hates the British is near. Will the girls see their father again?

There are hundreds of Penguin Readers to choose from – world classics, film adaptations, modern-day crime and adventure, short stories, biographies, American classics, non-fiction, plays ...

For a complete list of all Penguin Readers titles, please contact your local Pearson Longman office or visit our website.

www.penguinreaders.com

Pirates of the Caribbean
The Curse of the Black Pearl

Elizabeth lives on a Caribbean island, a very dangerous place. A young blacksmith is interested in her, but pirates are interested too. Where do the pirates come from and what do they want? Is there really a curse on their ship? And why can't they enjoy their gold?

Robin Hood

Robin Hood robbed rich people and gave the money to the poor. He fought against the greedy Sheriff of Nottingham and bad Prince John and defended the beautiful Lady Marian. *Robin Hood is a folk-hero and the story is supposed to be true!*

Matilda
Roald Dahl

When the headmistress attacks her, Matilda finds out she has extraordinary powers to protect herself. Now she isn't frightened of anyone! *Also a film starring Danny De Vito.*

Longman Dictionaries

Express yourself with confidence!

Longman has led the way in ELT dictionaries since 1935.
We constantly talk to students and teachers around the
world to find out what they need from a learner's dictionary.

Why choose a Longman dictionary?

Easy to understand

Longman invented the Defining Vocabulary – 2000 of the most
common words which are used to write the definitions in our
dictionaries. So Longman definitions are always clear and easy
to understand.

Real, natural English

All Longman dictionaries contain natural examples taken from
real-life that help explain the meaning of a word and show you
how to use it in context.

Avoid common mistakes

Longman dictionaries are written specially for learners, and we
make sure that you get all the help you need to avoid common
mistakes. We analyse typical learners' mistakes and include
notes on how to avoid them.

Innovative CD-ROMs

Longman are leaders in dictionary CD-ROM innovation. Did
you know that a dictionary CD-ROM includes features to help
improve your pronunciation, help you practice for exams and
improve your writing skills?

**For details of all Longman dictionaries, and to choose
the one that's right for you, visit our website:**

www.longman.com/dictionaries